In loving memory of all the slain black lives that mattered to someone yet they were taken from us way too soon. A small portion of each book sale will be donated to various foundations that aide in bringing change to our communities.
Special thanks to Alexis Ham

The police daddy, because I keep seeing them hurting black people every night when we watch the news. Well Quess, that's a very hard question to answer but you know what I will try to answer it the best way daddy knows how.   How daddy, with one of your bedtime stories right?
You guessed it my little smart cookie.

Long, long ago there was a kind and friendly koala by the name of Quess...
That's my name daddy!
I know Q, now let daddy finish the story please. Once long long ago, there was the most cutest, kindest kola named Quess and he loved to climb from tree to tree traveling the great big forrest. Mostly all of the animals of the forrest loved him and gave him great respect.

All except an owl by the named of Kevin that also traveled the forest. Kevin and his other owl friends didn't like Koalas very much.

But why daddy koala's are so adorable and loving?

Mostly because Kevin was afraid of Quess size he was so much bigger than owl was, then there was the fact that Quess was liked and respected by all the other animals.

That made Kevin feel sad and jealous that he didn't get the same love or respect from the other animals of the forrest.

One night while Quess was sitting way up on a high tree branch eating his food Kevin flew up to him and said "Your so big and clumsy I know you were the one that damaged my nest, your always climbing up trees destroying other owls homes. You should be ashamed of yourself."

Quess looked confused "I don't remember doing anything like that and if I did it was an accident and im very sorry, I could...."You could what? Your a big fat liar, that's all you are I'll fix you, you'll see."

And Just like that Kevin flew off.

Some of the other animals heard what happened and came to see if Quess was ok. Happily, Quess was fine but he was worried about what Kevin said before he flew off.

A few days had passed and nothing happened Quess traveled the forrest as he always did and everything was normal.

"Haa haaaha haaa, told you I would get you back, that'll teach you not to ever mess with me or my things again." Kevin had set a trap and Quess was tangled in it. The water from the rain was rising so fast.

Quess cried out "HELPP, SOMEBODY HELP ME, I DON'T KNOW HOW TO SWIM I CAN'T BREATH." Kevin stood there just watching as Quess was struggling to get free.

Just then Q's friend beaver overheard him screaming for help as he swam down to rescue him Kevin flu off again.

Early the next morning before the sun even rose Beaver went to talk to Kevin. Thump thump thump Beaver banged his tail at the bottom of the tree to get Kevin's attention.

"Why are you disturbing me? I have been protecting and hunting in the forest all night. I need my rest!" Shouted Kevin.

Beaver took a deep breath and nervously began to speak. "I am here an I thhiink I speak for most of the animals of the forest. We want to know why you dislike koalas so much."

Kevin shouts
"It's not your business, Beaver, now leave before me and my friends get angry!" Just then, two of Kevin's owl friends came from behind the leaves and stood next to Kevin. They tried to scare Beaver away.

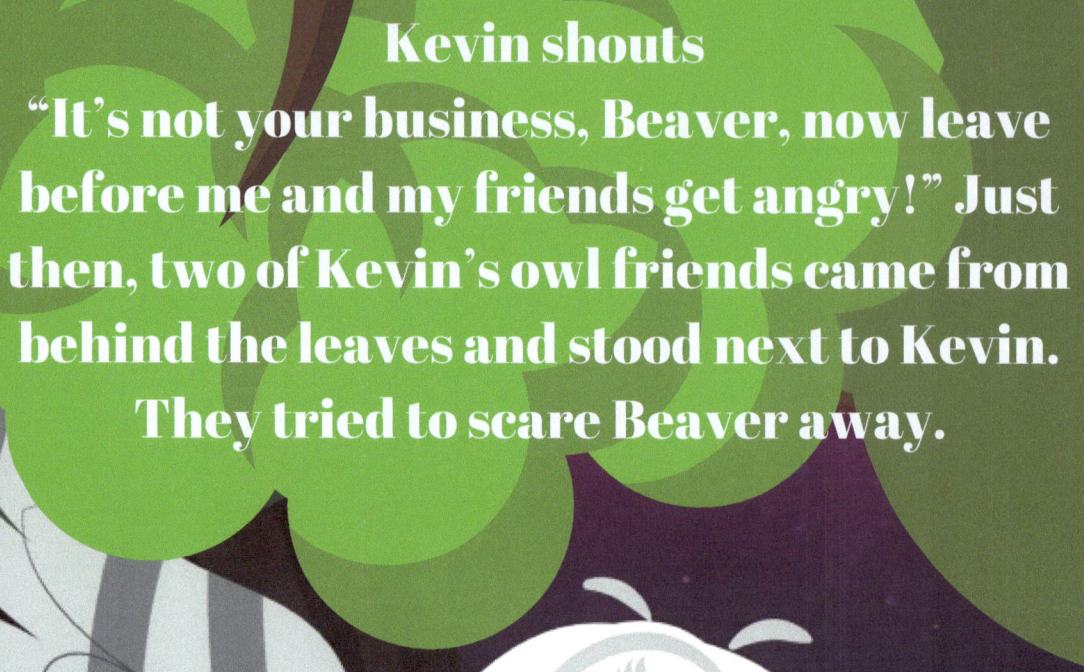

As Beaver stood there, wondering what to say next,
a few other animals started to pop out from every corner of the forest. Before Beaver knew it, animals of different shapes, size and species started marching out in larger numbers, even Quess showed up although he was pretty bruised up from his fall.

The animals all stood behind beaver in solidarity. Beaver started to feel much more confident and looked straight up into Kevin's eyes and said bravely, "THIS NEEDS TO STOP, it's not fair that the koalas and the other animals of the forrest have to live in fear of you and your owl friends!"

Just then every animal started shouting "No Unity No Peace." "No Unity No Peace." "No Unity No Peace." Kevin and his friends opened their eyes wide in shock. Kevin and his friends had never seen all of the animals of the forrest come together in unity like this to stand up to them before. In shock Kevin started to speak "You guys don't like us so why does it even matter."

"That's not true we don't dislike you'll, we just don't like when you and your friends do mean and hateful things to us!" exclaimed beaver.

Kevin just rolled his eyes and ruffled his feathers then he turned his back to the other animals as he laughed and said "Come on fellas let's get out of here its getting a little cramped, I don't think I can breathe now either."

When Quess heard him say it made him feel like Kevin was mocking him because that's the same thing he said when he was stuck in that trap he set for him earlier. It made Kevin think about how he almost drowned and that made him sad.

Beaver shouted "Kevin where are you going? You can't keep flying off like that your being a coward." Kevin and his friends didn't even give beaver or the other animals a second look as they flew off. Beaver turned to Koala and gave him a hug and said, "You know what Q you can't always reason with bullies."

"I'm sorry for what happened to you today but we all vow to make sure we look out for each other from now on, to make sure it doesn't happen again." The End.

Do you think the police are bullies like the Owls were in the story daddy? Well Q, I believe for the most part the police are good people that are here to help and protect us from bullies like the owl, but as you know there will always be a few bad apple mixed in with the good ones.

I believe those are the police that become bullies. Just like the animals of the forrest we all have to stick up for each other. Like when beaver was brave and stood up against the owl and his friends daddy?

Yes son exactly like that we have to stand up and stick together for all people of different colors and backgrounds to make sure a change happens so that bullies don't get mixed in with good police anymore. Eventually, when all the bullies of the world see that their behavior won't be tolerated they won't have any other choice but to stop. I love you daddy. I love you too son, now get some sleep, Goodnight. Goodnight daddy.

www.ingramcontent.com/pod-product-compliance
Lightning Source LLC
LaVergne TN
LVHW071030070426
835507LV00002B/92